Persecution Report from Markus Pilz

How Anabaptists are persecuted from the catholic and protestant church in the 21st century

Matthew 10:27

„What I tell you in darkness, *that* speak ye in light: and what ye hear in the ear, *that* preach ye upon the housetops.“

Imprint:
Media Owner / Place of Publication: Markus Pilz, Schildlehen 35, 8972 Ramsau am Dachstein
Manufacturer: Lightning Source LLC
Place of Manufacture: see imprint on the last page
Bible-Translation: King James Version

A Letter to the people of God in Babylon

I would like to tell you briefly my story, so that you may know what true Christians are like and how they fare in the 21st century and how they are persecuted and from whom and what is written about it in the Bible and where. It is a testimony of Jesus Christ.

At first you must know who the Antichrist is: Firstly, he has to come out of the Roman Empire, the last one that Daniel mentions, Daniel 7. Secondly, he has to sit „as God in the temple of God, shewing himself that he is God", 2. Thessalonians 2:4. Thirdly, the number of his name has to be counted together 666, Revelation 13:17-18. All these things apply to the pope as he comes out of the Roman Empire, he sheweth himself that he is God and his name, that is written on his crown (the Tiara), sums up in Roman letters to 666. Fourthly, he must kill the Christian for 1260 years, Revelation 12:6, and this applies also to the pope: from 538 where it truly began through Justinian until 1798 where Napoleon took the power from him. Fifthly does he not merely kill the Christians, but in advance he does not let them buy or sell, Revelation 13:17, which was always the case under the popery. In addition to this another institution like this has to do the same, Revelation 13, which applies to the protestant church. Here we already have the major points which can never all apply to anybody else except the pope. Because these things about the catholic and protestant church were prophecied so clearly and because it was not possible to exterminate the Bible, there remains only one possibility to deceive the world which is to conceal the murders of the catholic and evangelical church in the best way possible, namely, to lie about the victims or to keep silent altogether about these persecutions. This is being done all over the world to the most menial history-lesson in a village, everything intentionally and on purpose. Now I have discovered these things through the help of God and did say them on the Internet on YouTube and immediately after that the federal police (Austrian FBI) did come to me. It is written in the Bible, that „power was given" to the Antichrist „over all kindreds, and tongues, and nations", Revelation 13:7, and the kings of the earth work together with him, Revelation 17:2. This power was introduced already in the 7th century, thus they have this symbol of two keys: the earthly power and the spiritual power of the pope. Other synonyms for the Antichrist are „MYSTERY, BABYLON THE GREAT, THE MOTHER OF HARLOTS AND ABOMINATIONS OF THE EARTH", Revelation 17:5. This means that every evil on the earth comes from these two institutions, the catholic and evangelical church, and with „evangelical" I mean all those who have positive affections towards evangelical doctrine, even if they do not call themselves „evangelical". About the protestant or evangelical church - thereby I mean evangelicalism as a whole and those who teach evangelical ideas, therefore I mean almost every church that is not catholic - it is written in the Bible that their rulers are two people, Revelation 13:11, namely Luther and Calvin. This church looks like a lamb, but speaks as a dragon, Revelation 13:11. In addition it is written in the Bible, that „all that will live godly in Christ Jesus shall suffer persecution“, 2. Timothy 3:12, that means, that all who do not suffer persecution do not live godly in Christ Jesus. „Blessed are they which are persecuted for righteousness’ sake: for theirs is the kingdom of heaven“, Matthew 5:10. „Woe unto you, when all men shall speak well of you! for so did their fathers to the false prophets“, Luke 6:26. „Woe unto you that are full! for ye shall hunger. Woe unto you that laugh now! for ye shall mourn and weep“, Luke 6:25. Woe unto you, ye rich men! Your gold and silver will canker; and the rust of them shall be a witness against you, and shall eat your flesh as it were fire, James 5:3. Woe unto you if you come together cosily in your churches and do not have to fear death daily! Woe unto you who do not say a word against these two major churches! Woe unto you and your children after you! Woe unto you that read still and comfortably this book without standing out for me publicly! Woe unto you, ye miserable lukewarm creatures, that see the innocent suffer and shut up your bowels of compassion from them! Dear readers, do you think you can go on to live your life in this way and have no responsibility before God with this knowledge that you now have? And do you think you will be held guiltless if you break the command of Christ that saith: „Open thy mouth for the dumb in the cause of all such as are appointed to destruction“, Proverbs 31:8. What do ye think why Christ did say to his disciples: „Ye shall be hated of all nations for my name's sake“?, Matthew 24:9. Hath he not said: „Behold, I send you forth as sheep in the midst of wolves“?, Matthew 10:16. Do you think wolves merely insult sheep with words, or merely take away their working place? What do you mean Christ hath meant in the Greek when he saith, „they will deliver you up to the councils“?, Matthew 10:17. Do you mean that is to be taken symbolically, or that it was meant merely for the Christians at that time, or before Napoleon? Why did he say then these same words over and over, as on the mount of olives: „Then shall they deliver you up to be afflicted“, Matthew 24:9. Do you think you can read about persecutions calm and still without having to give an account before God and do you think, I can write this down unscathed without speaking to you directly through the Scriptures? What Christians are you? Enough said, you want to know how I am persecuted, I will tell you. It started in the Lutheran state church in Ramsau am Dachstein in Austria. As I found out that the Protestants are the so-called „beast of the earth“, Revelation 13:11, I said to everyone that it is a sin to go to that church or to be a member of it. After that it was forbidden to me to enter into their church building, although they knew that this Bible verse speaks about them. Then I was searching for the next-best church and found the reformed preacher from the US, Paul Washer. I flew to him and was directed to a reformed-baptist church in Germany (to Peter Schild and Co. who were 700 km away from me). I was baptized there, as I have been only sprinkled as an infant in the Lutheran church before, but I was excommunicated very quickly from their community, as I would restrict their freedoms too much because I do not drink and do not listen to rock music and so on. „While they promise them liberty, they themselves are the servants of corruption“, 2. Peter 2:19. The nearest next-best church was now in London, namely the church where Spurgeon preached. I spoke with the pastor and the elders there and they said that I should become a pastor to plant a church in Austria, which they say very rarely to someone. After that, the Holy Ghost called me to Ramsau and enabled me to do this, but completely different than this evangelical church in London, which is why I told them that all who follow murderers will be punished in hell as murderers, whereupon every contact with every member was forbidden to me, although they admitted that it is good for me, that God has blessed me with knowledge, and they said, that the Lord may bless my service for him, which is indeed nothing unusual for an evangelical church to approve of what I say and to tell me that I should continue my way without them. So far I did not have direct contact to a catholic church, which changed quickly after I posted videos on the Internet in 2021. There I called upon the rulers of all nations to forbid catholic and protestant churches, because genocidal traditions shall be forbidden. After that did the secret service come to me. They brought a picture with them about the part of my video where I say that the catholic church should be forbidden, because they always killed all Christians, and they also came because of the other sentence where I say the same thing about the evangelical church. They were very strange people which I have never met in my life before, neither seen performing in a movie. They were there for a very short period, about 10 to 15 minutes, I was not allowed to digress even one sentence without being rebuked very directly and very sharply not to digress and strangely they did not mention my criminal offense directly, but only said that these sentences (about the catholic and evangelical church) are against the law. But they did tell me two times explicitly that not only my doctrine, but also my life is „the truth". Although they admitted that it is the truth, they did say, it is forbidden to say that, whereupon I replied: „But it is the truth!", and they said: „Many things are the truth, but are forbidden." Our conversation was directed mainly just towards the murders of the catholic and evangelical church and it seems to me, even they did not say it expressly, that they did come, to find out from me personally how much I know about it and towards this direction were their questions formed. For me, it was afterwards quickly obvious, that these things that are written in the Bible about these two churches and about the rulers of all nations are being revealed in my life, namely, that they keep their machinations secret and eliminate all those, that stand up against them and these are always the Christians that stand up against them, in all ages and in all nations. They have told me that I should remove the videos and keep silent about it, but Christ saith about them: „What I tell you in darkness, that speak ye in light: and what ye hear in the ear, that preach ye upon the housetops", Matthew 10:27, and everyone that keeps silent is fearful and the „fearful" go to hell, Revelation 21:8, they deny Christ: „Whosoever therefore shall confess me before men, him will I confess also before my Father which is in heaven. But whosoever shall deny me before men, him will I also deny before my Father which is in heaven," Matthew 10:32-33. The true understanding of the Book of Revelation is the great secret of the two major churches and the Book of Revelation can be decoded very easily if one knows what these churches have done, and because they know that, they all do not talk about it and pretend to not understand the Book of Revelation, although they know that they themselves are meant therein. And this is the work of the Antichrist in all nations, therein they all covenanted together and „he who telleth it to them will be killed first", as the true Christians did sing and we continue to sing (see our hymnbook „Psalms, Hymns and Spiritual Songs" - Anabaptist Hymnbook, Markus Pilz). You may think I am selfwilled and have devised my own doctrine, but I merely follow in my doctrine the early Anabaptists, the victims of these churches, read my hymnbook, there the hymns of the martyrs are put together (translated from German into English) in which they expound these passages in the Book of Revelation. They were all of one mind. In addition, one major goal of the secret service is to find scriptural sins in us, because they did ask me if we sell alcohol. Now, everyone can see that selling alcohol is not a criminal act in Austria, and it is not the task of the secret service to punish that, but nevertheless they did ask me if our guesthouse does. Why? Very simple, because they want to depict us as sinners, so that also all other statements become untrustworthy, which is the case in all other churches that mention these murders, for which reason such churches do not represent any danger to the secret service. Therefore it is important that they persecute us „for righteousness' sake", Matthew 5:10, otherwise we would give our body to be burned, and have not charity, and become as sounding brass, or a tinkling cymbal, as Paul saith, 1. Corinthians 13:1-3. „He that hath my commandments, and keepeth them, he it is that loveth me", John 14:21, „For this is the love of God, that we keep his commandments", 1. John 5:3. The keeping of the commandments belongs together to the persecution and this does the secret service know and that is why he asks us about the alcohol. I told them that we as bed and breakfast do not serve alcohol whereupon the topic was off the table. This was namely the reason why I was excommunicated from one church, because I said that one should not sell alcohol to the guests, after which amongst others we do not offer dinner anymore. Now you know why you are not persecuted: either you do not preach the main sins of all nations upon the housetops, namely those of the catholic and evangelical church or you sin in another area. You have to do the one as well as the other and from such I and also others do not know in the last 200 years. Before Napoleon such people were everywhere in all nations for 1800 years and they were always everywhere persecuted to the uttermost. If they come to you merely with the normal police then it is not enough, they have to be the best forces and you have to be public enemy number 1 as the disciples of Jesus Christ have been always everywhere. It has been told to me by a lawyer very intensely, how it will end with people like me. He said that there are two possibilities: either I will be put to jail immediately for many years anyway and this because I do stand up against the catholic church, or they say they want to protect me from myself and put me into an institution. He also most intensely threatened that they transfer me to another country where I will be tortured, as it is written: „they will scourge you", Matthew 10:17. He said that it is clear how it will end up between me and the catholic church, namely 1-0 for them, and did say that he will not represent me, because I resist not evil and turn the other cheek also, Matthew 5:39. Which injections one gets in institutions for mentally deranged criminals should be clear to everyone and that this would surpass a death penalty even so. So far, so good, which path did my persecutors choose? Both, and this in the uttermost tempo, because at the place where it is written that „all that will live godly in Christ Jesus shall suffer persecution", 2. Timothy 3:12, there is meant with the word „persecution" in the Greek that they pursue you in haste. Generally, when „persecution" is written in the Bible, it is meant that they punish and exterminate you most quickly with all means available in the most severe way. No matter in which verse you look, you will find this word in this way except in the Letter to the Galatians where Ismael „persecuted" Isaac, Galatians 4:29. In any way, both things are always included, most severe persecution within the family so that they work together with them that want to kill you and pay those churches, as Christ saith: „And the brother shall deliver up the brother to death, and the father the child: and the children shall rise up against their parents, and cause them to be put to death", Matthew 10:21. And even if you plead with them most intensely not to support these churches after all and therefore securing them their only possibility for their existence, they do not only remain members, but pay the murderers of the prophets their livelihood, and this persecution within the family as also that from the state, that is meant in all verses in the New Testament, not merely mild disrespect against Christians. Paul says to the church of the Thessalonians that was persecuted exactly in this way: yourselves know that we are appointed to these afflictions", 1. Thessalonians 3:3. Christ saith: „Blessed are ye, when men shall revile you, and persecute you, and shall say all manner of evil against you falsely, for my sake. Rejoice, and be exceeding glad: for great is your reward in heaven: for so persecuted they the prophets which were before you", Matthew 5:11-12, therefore the persecution of the disciples of Christ has to be as severe as the persecution of the prophets. You want to read about my persecutions? Read those of the Apostle Paul and you know how we fare. Read the Bible, read about the prophets, read about Christ himself, then you know how we fare. It should suffice to simply list Bible verses to describe our persecution. And this I am doing, I list verses and tell you that we fare the like and nothing more. Who will lay a charge against this? Who will condemn us? Christ saith: „Ye shall be brought before governors and kings for my sake, for a testimony against them and the Gentiles", Matthew 10:18, which applies to us. Paul and Barnabas were „confirming the souls of the disciples, and exhorting them to continue in the faith, and that we must through much tribulation enter into the kingdom of God", Acts 14:22, and with „much tribulation" he meant the same as Christ and he said: „If any man will come after me, let him deny himself, and take up his cross daily, and follow me", Luke 9:23. Where did he go? Which cross? Do they want to kill you daily? Do the ungodly rejoice over you if you die and send gifts one to another?, Revelation 11:10. If not, you do not belong to the „two witnesses", as the true Christians are called in the Book of Revelation. Can the following paragraph be applied to you and your church, as Paul wrote it unto the church of God which was at Corinth: „But we have this treasure in earthen vessels, that the excellency of the power may be of God, and not of us. We are troubled on every side, yet not distressed; we are perplexed, but not in despair; Persecuted, but not forsaken; cast down, but not destroyed; Always bearing about in the body the dying of the Lord Jesus, that the life also of Jesus might be made manifest in our body. For we which live are alway delivered unto death for Jesus' sake, that the life also of Jesus might be made manifest in our mortal flesh. So then death worketh in us, but life in you. We having the same spirit of faith, according as it is written, I believed, and therefore have I spoken; we also believe, and therefore speak; Knowing that he which raised up the Lord Jesus shall raise up us also by Jesus, and shall present us with you. For all things are for your sakes, that the abundant grace might through the thanksgiving of many redound to the glory of God. For which cause we faint not; but though our outward man perish, yet the inward man is renewed day by day. For our light affliction, which is but for a moment, worketh for us a far more exceeding and eternal weight of glory; While we look not at the things which are seen, but at the things which are not seen: for the things which are seen are temporal; but the things which are not seen are eternal", 2. Corinthians 4:7-18. Paul saith: „we are made a spectacle unto the world, and to angels, and to men", 1. Corinthians 4:9, thus we sing in our 187th hymn, which was written according to the 111th hymn of the „Ausbund": „We have been made a spectacle to all the world." All spectate at us and no one helps us, as in the theater. Which letters did Paul not write in prison? „Paul, the prisoner of Jesus Christ", is written in Ephesians 3:1. He writes: „my bonds in Christ", in Philippians 1:13. To the saints which are at Colosse he closes with the words: „Remember my bonds", Colossians 4:18. In the Second Letter to Timothy Paul saith that he is the „prisoner" of the Lord, 2. Timothy 1:8. This is written as well at the beginning of the Letter to Philemon: „Paul, a prisoner of Jesus Christ", Philemon 1:1. Peter writes in his first letter to the scattered Christians the following: „And who is he that will harm you, if ye be followers of that which is good? But and if ye suffer for righteousness' sake, happy are ye: and be not afraid of their terror, neither be troubled; But sanctify the Lord

God in your hearts: and be ready always to give an answer to every man that asketh you a reason of the hope that is in you with meekness and fear: Having a good conscience; that, whereas they speak evil of you, as of evildoers, they may be ashamed that falsely accuse your good conversation in Christ. For it is better, if the will of God be so, that ye suffer for well doing, than for evil doing. For Christ also hath once suffered for sins, the just for the unjust, that he might bring us to God, being put to death in the flesh, but quickened by the Spirit", 1. Peter 3:13-18. He continues and writeth: „Forasmuch then as Christ hath suffered for us in the flesh, arm yourselves likewise with the same mind: for he that hath suffered in the flesh hath ceased from sin; That he no longer should live the rest of his time in the flesh to the lusts of men, but to the will of God", 1. Peter 4:1-2, and again: „Beloved, think it not strange concerning the fiery trial which is to try you, as though some strange thing happened unto you: But rejoice, inasmuch as ye are partakers of Christ's sufferings; that, when his glory shall be revealed, ye may be glad also with exceeding joy. If ye be reproached for the name of Christ, happy are ye; for the spirit of glory and of God resteth upon you: on their part he is evil spoken of, but on your part he is glorified. … Yet if any man suffer as a Christian, let him not be ashamed; but let him glorify God on this behalf", 1. Peter 4:12-14 and verse 16. That it was not much better in the Old Testament you can read in the

Psalms, all of which we do sing, because they are written in the same situation: Psalm 3: „LORD, how are they increased that trouble me! many are they that rise up against me", (verse 1). Psalm 7: „Save me from all them that persecute me, and deliver me", (verse 1). Psalm 118: „Princes have persecuted me without a cause", (verse 161). Why do ye think Christians shall sing all Psalms as it is commanded four times in the New Testament? Because they mirror the same situation as that of the believers of the New Testament. Do ye sing Psalms? Do ye sing songs that were written in the same situation as the Psalms? Or do ye sing lukewarm praises which were written by false Christians, who did not have death before their eyes daily for Christ's sake? These are no christian hymn writers, this is noise which the LORD will not hear, Amos 5:23. The Prequel of our hymnbook (the „Ausbund") was written mainly in prison in Passau in Germany in 1535-40 and it is the hymnbook that was used the longest in any christian tradition. These songs are well pleasing unto the Lord and Christians in such situations do sing such songs, as we do for example in the verse of our 168th song: „I'm salted with fire and the sufferings of Christ abound in me and I eat bitter Passah-herbs." Why do I tell you all these things? So that you may finally know, that we are not selfwilled and singular, but represent the doctrine of Christ and the Apostles, which was handed down over the centuries, and that all those things, which do happen now and today with Anabaptists in the 21st century, was the same fate of all Christians in all centuries. Now I do rather report about all other testimonies, embedding only portions of our story, so that you may know true Christianity, ye that hath such hardened hearts and that perceive so little! Do ye not see that Christ speaketh to you: „perceive ye not yet, neither understand? have ye your heart yet hardened?“ Mark 8:17. I do tell ye, as Paul doth: „Ye see how large a letter I have written unto you“!, Galatians 6:11. What do ye think why Christ saith: „Fear them not therefore: for there is nothing covered, that shall not be revealed; and hid, that shall not be known“, Matthew 10:26. Why doth he say this to his disciples? Obviously because the persecutors carry out their persecutions always as inconspicuously as possible, by wrongly accusing the Christians or if possible by keeping silent about the persecutions. All shall be revealed, I do not need to fear. And what do ye do that linger in lukewarm Babylonian churches? Do ye think it is easy to atone for the sins of others? Do ye even know that Christians do such a thing? Or have ye not read that Paul saith: „I … fill up that which is behind of the afflictions of Christ in my flesh for his body’s sake, which is the church“, Colossians 1:24? We have to atone for sins of other Christians, Christ hath not suffered for everything. Ye do not truly understand the atoning sacrifice of Christ, not even the milk of the word! „For when for the time ye ought to be teachers, ye have need that one teach you again which be the first principles of the oracles of God; and are become such as have need of milk, and not of strong meat. For every one that useth milk is unskilful in the word of righteousness: for he is a babe. But strong meat belongeth to them that are of full age, even those who by reason of use have their senses exercised to discern both good and evil“, Hebrews 5:12-13. „For whereas there is among you envying, and strife, and divisions, are ye not carnal, and walk as men?“, 1. Corinthians 3:3. You all still need milk and are not able to bear strong meat as the Corinthians, 1. Corinthians 3:2, and do not live separate, so that God hath not received you as children yet: „Wherefore come out from among them, and be ye separate, saith the Lord, and touch not the unclean thing; and I will receive you, And will be a Father unto you, and ye shall be my sons and daughters, saith the Lord Almighty“, 2. Corintians 6:17-18. Do ye not see that I merely cite the appropriate passages? Do ye not see that Peter in his second letter talketh about your teachers in your churches?, wherein he saith: „they speak great swelling words of vanity“, 2. Peter 2:18, „Having eyes full of adultery, and that cannot cease from sin; beguiling unstable souls: an heart they have exercised with covetous practices; cursed children“, 2. Peter 2:14, false teachers who are privily bringing in damnable heresies, even denying the Lord that bought them, 2. Peter 2:1, And through covetousness they make with feigned words merchandise of you,

2. Peter 2:3, „and bring upon themselves swift destruction“, 2. Peter 2:1, „whose judgment now of a long time lingereth not, and their damnation slumbereth not“, 2. Peter 2:3. Do ye not see, that you are still „children, tossed to and fro, and carried about with every wind of doctrine, by the sleight of men, and cunning craftiness, whereby they lie in wait to deceive“, Ephesians 4:14. But ye shall „come in the unity of the faith, and of the knowledge of the Son of God, unto a perfect man, unto the measure of the stature of the fulness of Christ“!, Ephesians 4:13. But ye are not able, because ye are in false churches. You do not think, that your teachers do intentionally deceive you, but a false doctrine does not happen accidentally. „The way of holiness“ of the New Testament, Isaiah saith, is so clear that even „fools shall not err therein“, Isaiah 35:8. Peter very well doth describe your churches, even if you think you were good people. The false preachers in the times of the Apostles appeared outwardly „righteous unto men“, as Christ hath said to the Pharisees, but within they are „full of hypocrisy and iniquity“, Matthew 23:28. Prove the opposite! Contact me! All churches - no matter which denomination - are false. Only one can be right, and only that tradition which always lived exactly the same life and had always the same doctrine, and only one tradition can prove this truly, even if all claim it for themselves. The Holy Ghost kept in all ages that good thing which was committed unto us, as Paul told Timothy,

2. Timothy 1:14. This I can prove through the whole works of Menno Simons, who stands in all points for the same doctrine with the same emphasis, choice of words and balances, all in all identical, although they are 800 pages. And I do not have my doctrine from „flesh and blood", Galatians 1:16, but learned it from God and found afterwards, not until „fourteen years after", Galatians 2:1, „by revelation" the works of this perfect teacher, who understands the milk and the meat and found for the first time „that gospel which I preach" Galatians 2:2, everything in exactly the same way as Paul saith about himself in the first two chapters of the Letter to the Galatians. Who ever teaches about these two chapters of Galatians and follows Paul therein? Nobody. I want you to come out of Babylon, as John saith: „Come out of her, my people, that ye be not partakers of her sins, and that ye receive not of her plagues", Revelation 18:4. I could write many things unto you about my persecutions, but I do not want to. If you want to know more, then come to me personally, I think nothing of impersonal instructions and look at my work as in vain, if no one contacts me. Did the Apostles write books and sat still in huge theological libraries? Do I want to claim that this is false? Yes, I do, for the only books that I do have on my shelf are the Bible and our hymnbook and two other books: one from Menno Simons containing the doctrine of Christ and Martyrs Mirror on the church-history of the true Christians, all other books I do not really need - phari-

saic babble. Come to us into the ark, Noah also was alone and „condemned the world“, Hebrews 11:7, and you know that on the last day it will be as in the days of Noah, Matthew 24:37. „When the Son of man cometh, shall he find faith on the earth?“, Luke 18:8.

Markus Pilz, pastor of the church of God in Ramsau am Dachstein in Austria